Do Case Studies have a Shelf Life?

Dr. Kisholoy roy

THIS BOOK IS DEDICATED TO ALL THE AFICIONADOS OF CASE STUDIES. TO ALL THOSE WHO LOVE READING, TEACHING AND LEARNING THROUGH CASE STUDIES. TO ALL THOSE WHO SINCERELY THINK ABOUT THE WELL BEING OF CASE STUDIES AND DO BELIEVE THAT CASE STUDIES ARE THE MOST POWERFUL LEARNING TOOL

Preface

Since the 1990s, emphasis on case based teaching has been on the rise as far as management education in India is concerned. In the global sphere too, such a shift in academic thought emerged at a similar juncture. Undoubtedly educational entities like the IIMs in India and Harvard, MIT and INSEAD have been pursuing this teaching methodology many years prior to the 90s but then case based teaching as a mainstream thought and practice was to be seen since the 1990s. One private university in India that effectively took the initiative to cultivate cases and promote case based teaching at a pan-India level has been the Icfai University. Its actions have propelled many other institutes and universities in the country to seriously and meaningfully pursue case development and teaching. One development that has really been in vogue for the last decade or so has been the organizing of case writing workshops and case competitions. I as a case writer, editor and teacher wholeheartedly welcome this development since first and foremost such events do make students think and do bring the teachers and students together on the platform of research where the minds mingle and the actual learning takes place. I strongly believe that if any institute wishes its students to nurture something called lateral thinking, it is case based learning that can really go a long way in fostering that strength. It is definitely one of the many and surest ways to make students industry ready in today's competitive sphere.

This book titled *Do Case Studies Have a Shelf Life* is extremely thought provoking to say the least. The very tenet on which this book is based is innovative and can incite look of debates and deliberations. It is best for anyone to consider this book as an accompaniment to my previously published book on case studies titled *How to Write and Teach Case Studies Effectively?* It has been phenomenally successful across the globe and i am confident that this book too will get its takers. Those who sincerely think about the well being of case studies as learning product and are evangelists of case based teaching and learning.

Apart from discussing about case studies and the way to design them, this book mentions about the elements that contribute to the shelf life of cases. It emphasizes on how to enhance the shelf life of case studies and how can not just the case writers and case development team but the marketing fraternity of cases and the teaching fraternity play a defining role in promoting and enhancing the shelf life of cases. The Concluding Thoughts on this topic hopefully shall invite various supporting and conflicting opinions and i as the author of this book will be interested to hear about them and respond. Readers of this book can therefore mail me their thoughts/views/opinions to scon60@gmail.com

Contents

Chapter 1

What are case studies?

- introduction to case studies
- designing case studies
- types of case studies

INTRODUCTION TO CASE STUDIES

Case studies are basically an account of a situation a company or an individual in a company is faced with and it serves as a trigger for effective conclusion of a situation, its analysis and recommendation of a suitable solution by its readers. Across learning domains be it engineering, medicine, psychology, information technology and of course management, case based learning have been in vogue for many years now and it is increasingly becoming a quintessential component of education since it makes students think, analyze and recommend and thus give them an opportunity to face simulated situations and redress the issues involved in that context. Textual learning is undoubtedly required but then it is this case based learning that makes students industry ready and confident individuals.

While case teaching or case based learning have become an integral part of management education (the focus of this book will be on that aspect primarily and examples in this book have been cited from the domain of marketing management only), there have been a number of organizations that have been devoting hours to develop appropriate case studies to be consumed by the students and teachers of b-schools. In many cases, we find both in India and in the global circuit that there are verticals within an educational entity that are concerned with the process of developing case studies. Examples in India like that Icfai Business School's divisions like IBS-CDC (Case

Development Center) and ICMR (Icfai Center for Management Research) or the case development wing of Amity University. Internationally examples of learning brands like Harvard Business School and INSEAD are well known to any individual concerned with case development and case consumption. Another interesting development that have taken place in recent years as far as development of case studies to be subsequently taken up for class discussions is concerned is the organizing of various case development workshops within and outside India where students and teachers from across verticals of management learning participate and develop case studies on the spot based on certain published sources or based on primary research. Such events have not contributed to the exchange of proliferation of creative management ideas among participants but also have contributed to the development of useful case studies to be taken up for class discussions across institutes of the country.

Coming back to the aspect of defining case studies, one first needs to differentiate between case studies or rather business case studies and business articles. Often we come across articles in business newspapers and magazines that seem to be thought provoking and capable of inviting or inciting decisions but then it is the structure and approach to case development that differentiates case studies from articles (often both are developed from secondary sources or in other words from published sources). Primarily, case studies are dispassionate in the way they treat or project a situation. They are a dispassionate commentary of a business situation that calls for effective understanding, analysis and decision making. A case writer unlike an author of an article should not be opinionated in his/her expressions while writing a case. He/she should not influence the readers in any form towards making a certain decision; rather should provide an understanding of a concept, situation so that the reader can make a well informed decision and not a biased one. An effectively written case should contain various debatable issues surrounding a situation which can be suitably discussed and brainstormed before arriving at a logical conclusion in forums like classes and panel discussions.

DESIGNING CASE STUDIES

Coming to the structure or format, case studies have number of elements that differ from an article. To start with, the title of a case study should be as informative as possible yet it should not be an 'endless saga'. The title should ideally say what the reader can expect to come across in the case study. It should specify the core theme of a case and there are many case titles that spark a debate right at the outset. One of my very first case studies that i wrote as a professional was based on McDonald's and it was titled: "*McDonald's Localization Strategy: Brand Unification, Menu Diversification?*" [Case Reference: 306-316-1]. This case study is available on http://www.thecasecentre.org

Now here you can see that the case title not only provides information about what you can expect to come across in this case study but it also offers room for debate. Is it the same American look and feel whenever you visit a McD's at any place in the world? Are the items of the menu really differentiated in tune with the province where an outlet exists? What are the elements that are same about this fast food giant across continents and countries and what are those elements that keep changing? So this is what is a complete, informative case title that offers sufficient motivation to debate, brainstorm and reach conclusions. In this context, a title for an article could well have been mentioned as "*McDonald's Across Continents*" or for that matter a more fashionable title could have been "*McDonald's: Serving America in Different Platters*".

Another important aspect to be noted in terms of format of case studies especially those composed from secondary or published sources is that before the case introduction section there is something called an opening quote in a case study which should be summarizing the core theme of a case. This opening quote should ideally come from some individual of authority in an organization or industry and should have the content within it to encapsulate the entire flavour of a case. Often when we talk of inspiring debates through a case, we come across two such opening quotes with distinctly different thoughts that expose the debate right at the outset. The opening quotes are also often used to reinforce the core purpose of a case. Continuing with the

McDonald's example that i have cited before, there were two opening quotes to reinforce the point of localization as you can see over here:

"McDonald's was built on a strong foundation of a core menu that we took around the world but we need to make sure we are more locally relevant" – Ken Koziol

"*The world is getting smaller and flavours are travelling.*" – Dan Coudreaut

Similarly coming to the aspect of conflicting thoughts being shared right at the outset of a case, let me cite the example of another case study of mine titled: "*Indian Television's Music Reality Shows: Ephemeral Fame Providers or Enduring Career Launchers?*" [Case Reference: 506-118-1; available with The Case Centre]. Over here, take a look at the two opening quotes to have a better understanding –

"A talent show is now the starting point of a singer's career, it gives you the guarantee of a career." – Nikhil Alva

"You might get your first break easily but after that it's an uphill task." – Sanjeevani Bhelande

A business article will hardly have anything like this ever. Yes we often come across certain snapshots here and there highlighting few major and defining sentences within the article but then such are not to be considered as opening quotes.

Following opening quotes comes the section where a case reader wishes to learn about the case study in a nutshell and it is generally the 'introduction' section of a case study that serves this requirement. It places a case study within a certain time frame/context and details briefly about what can the reader expect to come across within the case study. Often certain important questions are raised over here which obviously has answers within the case study as one goes deeper into it. For example the introduction section of the case study titled: "*Baahubali: The Beginning – Digital Marketing Strategies*" [Case code: 516-0108-1]; available with www.The Case Centre.org], the case writer raises some extremely pertinent questions at the end of the introductory section of the case like:

- How did the movie turn from a 'yet another regional movie' into a magnum opus?
- What made the movie an epic blockbuster?
- How was the production company successful in its promotional campaigns and how did it manage to get huge publicity for the film that contributed to its commercial success?

Here is an example of a typical introductory section of a case study which should be brief, to the point and encapsulate the overriding idea of a case being presented. This section has been taken from one of my authored case studies titled *PVR Cinemas: Competitive Strategies of the Indian Cineplex Pioneer* [Case Code: COM0118; available with ibscdc.org].

[PVR, the largest cinema exhibition company in India, pioneered the multiplex concept in the country. With the launch of its first multiplex, PVR Anupam, in Saket, New Delhi(the national capital of India), PVR redefined the cinema viewing experience in India with comfortable seating arrangement, state-of-the-art screens and superior audio visual systems. The company, which started its commercial operations in 1997, has expanded to other areas in New Delhi, the National Capital Region (NCR) of India, Bangalore (a southern city) and some other prominent cities of India. In 2003-2004, PVR had a turnover of INR 63 crore and it is expected to rise to INR 350 crore (INR stands for Indian National Rupee. 1$= INR 44.89 as on May 10th 2006) by 2008. During the first three quarters of the FY 2005-2006, PVR entertained 6.5 million cine goers.

In February 2006, PVR Cinemas added another multiplex to its existing chain by launching a five-screen facility at Hyderabad (Capital of Andhra Pradesh, a South Indian state). The company has sixty two screens at sixteen locations in India as of May 2006. It has been observed that since the beginning of the 21st century, the multiplex business has attracted both real estate developers, who want to add value to their existing business, and other businessmen who have excess cash in hand. PVR faces competition from multiplex operators like Fame, Adlabs, Inox and Fun, who are foraying into smaller towns of India with diverse offerings apart from establishing themselves in the metros. Industry observers believe that Ajay Bijli (Bijli), the CEO and managing director of PVR, needs to make some strategic moves to fend off competition. The general feeling is that Bijli is capable of out playing competitors as he had been instrumental in ushering in a revolution in the Indian cinema exhibition industry.]

The section that succeeds the introductory section often speaks of the background of a company or rather the origin of a company and its evolution over the years or let's say if the case study is based on any movie this section might speak of other movies released in the past of similar genre and the audience reaction to such movies. The moot point is that the second section of any case study often takes the reader on a retrospective ride only to make him/her understand and appreciate the relevance and the contextual settings of the case study.

It is often the third section of the case that is the focal point of the case. It contains the main theme of the case study and discusses the issues and events that need prime attention. The rule of the thumb in case study development says that this section should at least range from 60% -75% in terms of length. In other words, if there is a case study of

10 pages length, this section should be 6-7 pages lengthwise.

The final section of a case study often takes a futuristic look like which way a company is heading or what challenges can the company expect to face in future. This section often talks of the controversies or the vulnerable areas so that the decision making or the case assessment being made is more informed and pertinent.

TYPES OF CASE STUDIES

Case studies can be of various types depending on various parameters. To start with, let's look at the various **specialization verticals** on which case studies are developed:

- Case studies on Marketing
- Case studies on Finance
- Case studies on Human Resources
- Case studies on General Management
- Case studies on Business Strategy
- Case studies on Media Management

Case studies are classified based on **target audiences**:

- For MBA students (length of cases generally ranging from 10-25 pages)

- For BBA students (length of cases generally ranging from 4-8 pages)
- For business executives (length of cases generally ranging from 3-6 pages)

- For recruitment purposes of content writers etc (length of cases are generally short of 1-2 pages)

Case studies are classified based on the **presentation of case content**:

- Paragraph wise presentation in textual format
- Power point presentation highlighting objectives/problem and solutions (refer to annexure for further understanding)
- Textual presentation in the form of dialogues

Case studies are classified based on **triggers involved**:

- Story driven cases (based on newspaper and magazine reports)
- Concept driven cases (based on a theoretical concept like second-mover advantage)

Case studies are classified based on **approach to case development**:

- Case studies based on field/primary/empirical research
- Case studies based on secondary research/published sources

Chapter 2

What is the case development process?

- Identifying triggers for a case
- Components of a case study
- Testing of a case in class
- Uploading cases

Identifying triggers for a case

The case development process starts with identifying suitable base articles (in case of case studies developed from published sources) or identifying significant business developments on the business horizon (national and international) (in case of case studies developed through field research). As an individual serving at the helm of case development affairs in any institution he/she should ideally conduct a suitable brainstorming session with case writers and case supervisors to understand the efficacy of a topic and the mileage the same can gain in the market in terms of visibility and sales once the case is published. After all case development has a business motive and is not something solely creative where one just writes something about which one is passionate about. The cases should be read, appreciated, purchased and as far as possible significant WoM (word of mouth) needs to be generated among the academic fraternity for a case to be more durable in its existence.

In case of case studies developed from published sources, once the theme of a case or the main idea of a case study is zeroed upon, search for a suitable article is the next step which can serve as the base article for the case study. The reason why it is called the base article is this one article should be providing maximum fodder for thought to the case writing team working on a case regarding the context and structure of a case. It should serve as a spinal chord for the development of a case. In the context of my case study titled *"McDonald's Localization Strategy: Brand Unification, Menu Diversification?"*, the article titled *"Golden Arches bridge local tastes"* by Jeremy Grant served as the base article for the case study. Once you read this article and then read the case study, you will understand the essence of a base article and its utility in the development of a case. One thing thus to be religiously kept in mind is that identifying the base article or the trigger for a case is of paramount importance and so sufficient amount of time and labour needs to be devoted to identify one such article on a topic and theme. Care should be taken to seek articles from such authentic sources that are largely recognized and approved by the world of academics like *Financial Times, The Wall Street Journal, The Economist, The Economic Times, Business Standard* etc.

Components of a case study

Much has already been discussed about how to design case studies and the various sections of a case study. As mentioned, there is an opening quote or quotes in a case study followed by the Introduction section, the background note etc. There are certain elements like Exhibits and Annexure that are integral part of a case study and so are footnotes or endnotes in a case. Exhibits are to be found within the text of a case while Annexure come at the end of a case. Source of an exhibit is mentioned below an exhibit and in cases where an exhibit is compiled from various sources, '*Compiled by the author*' is mentioned below the exhibit.

Footnotes basically talk of sources from where the various information for a case study have been collated and they follow a certain styling as mentioned below:

For authored articles sourced from offline sources like newspapers the following footnote styling is used –

Surname of author, first name of author, "Title of article", name of publication (in italics), Page number (s), Date of publication (format to be followed: July 25th 2015)

For authored articles sourced from online sources the following footnote styling is used –

Surname of author, first name of author, "Title of article", complete URL of the article, Date of publication (format to be followed: July 25th 2015)

For information/concept taken from books the following footnote styling is used –

Surname of author, first name of author, name of the book (in italics), Page number (s), Edition, year of publication

For information/concept taken from journals the following footnote styling is used –

Surname of author, first name of author, "Title of article", Volume number (Issue number), Page number (s), Date of publication

Once a case study is completed in all respects and it is approved by the case team, it is essential to develop certain add on materials for the case study for enhanced understanding both for teachers administering a case in class as well as for students in class. One such add on material is Structured Assignment which has a set of questions based on the case study that facilitate analytical thinking in students and enables them to dissect a case effectively. Another add on material is Teaching Note which is meant for teachers and this basically guides as how to administer a case in class. Both structured assignments and teaching notes mention additional readings that help teaching and student community to get better grasp of case studies, their concepts and their central themes. The add on materials are available along with case studies on various online repositories like www.The Case Centre.org and http://ibscdc.org/

Testing of a case in class

Case study repositories like The Case Centre make it mandatory that a case study should be tested in class regarding its efficacy before being uploaded on the site or before being submitted for upload. I as a case writer, case editor and as a teacher totally committed to case based teaching do subscribe to this practice. When a team comes together to develop a case, they are mainly researching on a topic, collating the data and information available and then weaving them in a way that develops into an informative and engaging read. But then when case studies are being developed mainly for the consumption of students at b-schools, you need to understand how far a developed case study is being assimilated and accepted by the target audiences before the same getting published.

It should be seen that the case study being taken to a class for class testing purpose is relevant to the audience in terms of assimilation and appreciation. If i take a case study on working capital management in a class of Marketing specialization, i am not doing justice to anyone. Similarly if i take a case study on celebrity endorsements and brand communications in a class Finance specialization similar will be the opinion. You need to take the correct case to the correct audience to understand the pulse of target group regarding how easy is the case to understand and dissect for solution. The size of the class also matters in this case. A minimum of 25-30 students is what is required to understand the vibes regarding a case. Also the class testing of a case does not restrict a teacher to administer a case only once in a class. The more a case is tested for efficacy across classes the better will be the understanding of how effective or ineffective is a case study meant and developed for a certain class of students. Also it will give a clearer understanding as to how far the pedagogical objectives have been addressed through the case study.

It is this general practice of class testing of case studies because of which we often find that organizations meant for case development are housed within an institute or learning organization or are a related SBU of a b-school which again is part of a larger corporate brand. Case development organizations like IBS-CDC and ICMR are part of Icfai Business School. Then again an organization like ET Cases is an SBU of the Times Group; whose output (case studies, structured assignments and teaching notes) are being consumed by the b-school of Bennett University (established by the Times Group).

Uploading cases

In this section, i will strictly be restricting my thoughts to The Case Centre since that happens to be the largest and the most popular case repository in the world. It is one platform where some of the world's best and classic case studies can be found and it also has a host of resources on case development and encouragement for case development that are rich in content. There are several case competitions and case training programs that are organized by the resource people at the organization for case studies to prosper or flourish in the world of academics. The organization is largely UK based but then it has offices in the US and other representative member bodies in various countries of the globe.

The case authors submitting case studies to The Case Centre can be assured of greater visibility of their work worldwide as teachers, researchers and corporate entities do visit this site in large numbers. Academic institutions around the globe are generally found to be members of The Case Centre. Individual memberships are not offered by the organization. One needs to be a corporate entity to qualify getting royalties from case purchases. Individuals too can submit cases but then they do not qualify to get royalties.

However coming to the issue of case uploads, there are certain requirements to be fulfilled before a case can be successfully uploaded on The Case Centre site. Case studies being uploaded should have proper Abstracts along with Pedagogical objectives are developed and these will serve as 'lead magnet' [a terms borrowed from the subject of digital marketing] for a case being uploaded. Potential buyers of case studies will go through the abstracts and the objectives to take a call on buying a case and hence these should be clearly and comprehensively described so that all the selling points of a case study are highlighted and optimal sales of a case happen.

At The Case Centre, a case study is considered ready for submission and distribution only when it has been comprehensively tested in a classroom. Now this issue of class testing has just been dealt with in the previous section. While filling out the details in the submission form, the following details are to be mentioned regarding class testing of a case:

- Course title on which the material was taught
- Name of the institution where it was taught
- Name of the teacher who taught it
- Date when it was taught
- Number of students present in the class when it was taught

A case study must have been taught at least two times before it is to be submitted for upload.

The Case Centre.org makes it mandatory to submit cases as case packs wherein a case study is accompanied with a suitable teaching note and a structured assignment. These two have already been mentioned about in detail in one of the previous sections in this book. In case of case studies developed through field study, a signed permission from the subject organization must accompany the case upload documents. An extract of a sample letter seeking permission from a subject organization has been provided below:

I very much appreciate your co-operation over the past few weeks in allowing me to talk to you and your staff about the restructuring you have recently implemented within the company. On the basis of these discussions and the documents you kindly provided, we have prepared the attached case entitled '................' . I hope this reflects the key issues that you had to address without revealing any confidential information. We believe the case will make a valuable contribution to the teaching of ... on our courses.

When you have noted any final corrections you wish me to make will you please sign and return one copy of this letter to indicate your agreement to publication of the case and its distribution by The Case Centre for educational use.

Signed: Position: Date:

CDs, DVDs and downloadable files are accepted for distribution by The Case Centre but then multimedia items cannot be hosted online by the site.

Once a case pack is successfully submitted/uploaded, an individual case reference number is assigned which is used throughout the database and for ordering. Bibliographical details of the case are available in the online search data base of The Case Centre and an Inspection Copy of a case is uploaded for potential customers to view. Educators across the globe have access to inspection copies of teaching notes too.

Chapter 3

Do case studies have a shelf life?

- Defining shelf life of case studies
- Enhancing shelf life of cases

What is shelf life of a case study? Do case studies have something called a shelf life? Well, i have an answer to both the questions. By shelf life we mean a time period within which a case is found to be effectively functioning; it is effectively serving as a learning and application tool within the framework of a particular course. The utility of a case study is felt both by the students and the teachers each time it is administered in a relevant class.

Coming to the second question, we do appreciate the fact that books have a shelf life and that's exactly why authors go for additions and improvisations to a book from time to time. Time changes, attitude to teaching and learning changes, the business environment changes, the trends change and so learning materials also need improvisations. But then in case of books, there are books that enjoy a longer shelf life while there are some which move out of the market within a matter of few years. Amends are required and are made to almost every book till such time the author(s) of a book are alive or the publishing entity survives. Often even if the original publishing entity gets acquired by some other publishing brand, that brand ensures the continuity of certain books. However, as i was stating that there are books that enjoy longer shelf life; a longer life of relevance and utility. Take the case of Marketing Management by Philip Kotler or the Strategic Brand Management by Kevin Keller. These two are undoubtedly two of the longest surviving books in the international learning arena as far as the domain of the Marketing Management is concerned. Improvisations have been made to these from time to time but then if you take a closer look, more than 90% of the original content is still intact in these which influences us to understand that any creative activity in the context of learning or otherwise requires vision. The vision to look beyond the obvious, the vision to include content and present the content in such a way that it transcends time and geographic boundaries and in due course of time become gospels to be religiously followed.

So here, i have mentioned two very important ingredients that can enhance the shelf life of any reading or learning material viz. content and presentation. In today's digital marketing arena, you can call content king, queen, slave or whatever you feel like but then the fact remains that content can make or break any and every thing in this world. What we say, what we do, what we see; everywhere the content is of paramount importance and if that goes for a toss, the entire thing is gone.

Case studies are learning materials, application based tools; they are something that reinforces the substance one learns as a student in the theoretical classes. However we often find academicians taking 'dead cases' to a class. A case study that talks of the strategic battle between Ambassador and the Premier Padmini in India way back in the 1970s and early 80s is one such example. The central theme of such a case has lost its relevance long back. Similar will be the case for a case study that details the competitive strategies of Nirma and Surf. The subject matter of a case or the pedagogical objectives are not enough qualify the suitability of a case to be discussed in a class of today. The content in them is one primary aspect to be considered. The brands being mentioned in the case study should ideally be existing when a case is being discussed so that students can assimilate the case suitably and can bring their thoughts to work as far as case analysis is concerned. The same holds true even for concept based cases.

Unlike books, the authors of case studies often do not keep getting royalties. Rather royalties as such are not associated with case authors and hence once a work is done, for certain obvious and logical reasons, improvisations to that very case cannot be made with passage of time.

Enhancing shelf life of cases

I just mentioned about concept based cases couple of sentences back and coming back to that context i will like to cite the example of an authored case of mine titled: "*LOWE'S, AMD, TARGET ET AL: The Second-Mover Advantage?*" [Case Reference: 306-329-1; available with http://www.thecasecentre.org]. The theoretical concept inspiring this case in the year 2006 was second mover advantage but this case qualifies to be one to be carried to marketing and strategy classes even today because the brand names mentioned or the corporate entities mentioned are all alive and kicking today. They are relevant and students with some additional research work triggered by the structured assignments and teaching notes accompanying this case can derive wholesome learning. So here i have just provide the first example of enhancing shelf life of case studies.

My next case example is another self authored one available with The Case Centre titled "*McDonald's Localization Strategy: Brand Unification, Menu Diversification?*"[Case reference: 306-316-1]. Take a look at the abstract in the Annexure section of this book to understand how content can enhance shelf life of a case. This case not only deals with an evergreen topic of localization or shall i say 'glocalization' but then the localization measures of McD's are there in front of everyone. One can experience the brand any day anywhere and appreciate the relevance of the content of the case. With additional and updated research further value can be added by teachers in a class on marketing and strategy.

My next self authored case example available with The Case Centre titled: "*Indian Television's Music Reality Shows: Ephemeral Fame Providers or Enduring Career Launchers?*" [Case Reference: 506-118-1]. The abstract can be referred to in the Annexure section but then over here, it should be pretty evident to any Indian living in India or abroad both Indian music reality shows as well as their purpose or rather their effectiveness in introducing new singing talents to the industry is something open to debate and that makes this case written again some 12 years back extremely relevant even today and again over here that a little research work done by both students and teachers administering this case in class of media and television students can make some definite value additions to this case and can thus benefit wholesomely from it. There have been plenty of faces and voices that have been launched through singing reality shows in India over the years gone by. Sunidhi Chauhan, Shreya Ghoshal, Monali Thakur and Arijit Singh are some brighter stars to be named over here. There have been many who won singing contests but then they were nowhere to be found later on or they did not stay in limelight for long. Again there have been voices like Arijit Singh, Monali Thakur and Neha Kakkar who could not make much headway in a singing reality show but then they emerged later on as singing sensations of the country. So the very efficacy of music reality shows in launching sustainable careers is a topic of debate and interest.

Any case analysis and discussion process in class is but a communication activity where both the teacher and students should have a definite purpose towards fulfilling a learning requirement and thus the good old AIDA model serves well to guide a case writer towards developing cases with enhanced shelf life rather than developing cases that will sustain short term interest and relevance.

For enhanced shelf life of case studies, a case writer should fulfil the following requirement. First and foremost, the case study should be attention grabbing and over here, the title of the case, the way it is constructed and the content of the title are of great importance. Next the Abstract and pedagogical objectives of the case study should be interesting. It should make a potential reader or potential buyer crave to go through the case in detail. An extract of a case should create further desire to go for purchase (action). If the case is already available in totality, the case should trigger in action in terms of making the case readers attempt the structured assignments, go for additional reading materials mention over there and thus imbibe wholesome learning through the case.

It's now high time to clarify something. A case with enhanced or low shelf life is not equivalent to a good or bad case. The issue of shelf life has not much to do with whether a case has been nicely written or not at least for me since a bad case or a wrongly structured or composed case anyway does not stand a chance to be purchased or touched even. A case may be nicely written but the central theme often restricts it from being a material that can be considered useful for times to come.

Consider the following case studies of mine:

- *The Namesake: The Success Recipe oj an Indian Crossover Movie*
- *MojoPac: Redefining Mobile Computing?*
- *Chak De! India: A Sustainable Trendsetter or an Ephemeral Euphoria?*
- *PepsiCo's `Youngistaan' Advertisement : Another Trendsetter in the Youth Marketing Arena*

The above cases are available on my blog: http://casestudiesandarticles.blogspot.in/ Some of them are available with the ibscdc.org site and with the Icfai University Press site (iupindia.in). I have had several class tests of each of these cases in the past and each of them have emerged with flying colors as far as ease of comprehension and analysis is concerned but then due to the subject matter or central theme of the case, i personally do not find much relevance of bringing those cases of mine in a class today. There have been several crossover movies post the Namesake and there have been more valid and contemporary recipes that have come to the forefront. So how can the case remain relevant today? How can a case on mobile computing technology written way back in 2006 remain interesting and attention grabbing today? Forget about creating desire and action!! There have been several Indian movies after Chak De! India that have brought about changes in the societal behaviour and outlook so why will people like to go back to doing a post mortem of a movie that released a decade back? Again Pepsi, the youth centric brand has come up with several engaging campaigns post Youngistaan that released in 2008.

A self authored and immensely popular case study of mine on celebrity endorsements was developed way back in 2007. It was titled *"Celebrity Popularity and Brand Endorsements: Understanding the Correlation through the Sourav Saga"* [available on my blog: http://casestudiesandarticles.blogspot.in/]. Sourav Ganguly is someone who is a well known and respectable figure in the game of contemporary Indian cricket. First and foremost the title thus is attention and interest grabbing. Secondly it talks of a phenomenon that is and will stay relevant till the last day we hear about celebrity endorsements on this earth. Brands wish to associate with celebrities who are in the limelight, who are popular and those who can offer a positive rub-off effect to brands which enable them to seek greater mileage in the over-crowded market. Brands come like a swarm of bees when someone is at the peak in terms of popularity and performance (more so in case of athletes) and leave in a similar fashion when they encounter a sorry phase in their career. This case thus although written a decade back stays relevant to be taken up for purposeful discussion and analysis even today in a class of marketing while dealing with issues like brand communication and celebrity endorsements.

Before concluding this most pivotal chapter in this book, i will like to bring forth another important aspect regarding shelf life of cases. Apart from content and presentation of content in case studies along with of course their central theme it is return on investment of efforts that go into developing case studies that also determine shelf life of cases. Apart from money, it is the appreciation, interest, word of mouth generated, number of clicks recorded for cases uploaded in online repositories that count for shelf life of cases. Hence over here, the fraternity concerned with case marketing at various organizations have an important role to play for maximizing the visibility of cases. They should be segmenting the potential market suitably and then go for innovative measures in promoting the case studies to the right set of audiences so that the right cases get noticed by the right target segment and desired action/response do take place. Just like any other product, case studies too are products that require effective positioning so that certain case studies are etched suitably in the mind of target audience and they do generate suitable recalls at suitable juncture. In today's era of digital marketing, innovative marketing practices do have significant scope in the context of case promotions. What effective marketing practices can ensure is that even if a case has limited shelf life because of its central theme or any other reason, it still can generate significant positivity in terms of its reach and purpose within a time frame. The teaching and research fraternity of course plays a defining role by generating suitable word of mouth among their peer groups. They will be treated as credible ambassadors when it comes to promotion of cases.

Chapter 4

Concluding thoughts

There's a saying in English – "*All good things must come to an end*" which was supposedly coined by a gentleman named Geoffrey Chaucer in 1374. Over here i will take a little bit of liberty in distorting this saying. I say – *All good things do come to an end.* What i mean to say is that all good case studies will have a shelf life. There is no product in this world that can have an eternal shelf life since products are used by consumers and consumers are humans who keep evolving with the passage of time in terms of knowledge, understanding, requirement, technology usage, interests and desires etc. There can be a classic case on Coca Cola written way back in the 1960s. It can be a case that was awarded and highly appreciated over the years but then i can hardly contemplate any case written in that era that can be brought to a class of management students today. Harvard Business School has been for decades one of the brightest stars as far as case development in global arena is concerned but then even they will appreciate the fact that no case of theirs can be considered to have an eternal shelf life. Case studies are products which cannot be equated with Holy grails like The Bible, Quran, The Bhagvad Gita etc that have ardently followed, read and appreciated for centuries together across generations and continents.

As mentioned earlier, when i talk of shelf life of cases, bad cases or cases developed inefficiently and ineffectively do not feature anywhere on the horizon. I am interested about talking good cases but then i have already mentioned ways and means of enhancing their shelf life. There will be certain aspects in this context that have to be taken care by the case writer and the case development team and then there are aspects to be looked into by the marketing team and the teaching fraternity. To start with, the teaching fraternity should first and foremost actively adopt case based teaching across institutions and case discussions in class need to be more thought provoking and engaging rather than simple 'reading comprehension' type sessions which are usually mundane affairs. Better branding around cases should be pursued by the marketing fraternity. Just like Sunsilk 'Gang of Girls' happened around the brand or around brands like Harley Davidson, communities need to be developed around outstanding cases so that they get the necessary attention and mileage and do not just get limited to few academic networks only.

Shelf life of case studies can surely be extended and there are innovative ways of doing that especially in this era of digital marketing. There is so much of media convergence happening due to technology and the target audiences can be reached through multiple channels and means. Communities around case repositories like The Case centre are a good way of developing loyal base of customers for cases and triggering positive word of mouth for various case studies. Also effective email marketing tools can see to it that information regarding quality case studies reach out to relevant target markets so that desired responses can be generated.

Annexure

- Case abstracts
- power point presentation of case highlighting objectives and solutions

Case abstracts

Certain case studies have been cited as examples within the chapters of this book. Abstracts of those along with corresponding case references have been mentioned over here for readers to pursue reading the complete case studies (either by ordering them or going through the inspection copies of the cases at **The Case Centre**). Some of the case study resources are also available on my blog titled *http://casestudiesandarticles.blogspot.in/*

McDonald's Localization Strategy: Brand Unification, Menu Diversification? **[Case Reference: 306-316-1]**

Abstract:

McDonald's, the world's leading fast-food retailer with 30,000 restaurants in 119 countries, has successfully maintained its global brand identity by standardising its principles and service quality, but customising its offerings across the globe. The highlight of McDonald's localisation strategy has been its foray into Asia where it has survived and has repeatedly proved itself vis-a-vis other big food retailers who have failed due to their inability to adapt to Asia's diverse cultures, tastes and temperaments. The case is structured to enable students to: (1) understand the importance of adaptation to local culture, tastes and preferences for global food retailers; (2) understand how McDonald's has maintained uniform brand identity across the globe while customising its menu to suit local tastes; and (3) analyse whether McDonald's localisation strategy would prove to be a disadvantage if the brand loses its unique American appeal. A structured assignment is available to accompany this case.

***Indian Television's Music Reality Shows: Ephemeral Fame Providers or Enduring Career Launchers?* [Case Reference: 506-118-1]**

Abstract:

Since 1995, music reality shows have become an important part of Indian television programmes. These shows received a major boost in 2003 due to the advent of media convergence that enabled television channels to transform their shows into interactive ones where the audience, through their votes over emails or SMS' (short message services), could decide the winners of these shows. Although this ensures instant recognition for the winners, the sheer number of upcoming talents spawning out of these shows has led to uncertainty about the future of their careers in the Indian music industry. The teaching objectives are: (1) to understand the concept of reality shows and how they differ from normal television programmes; (2) to analyse the reasons behind the evolution and rapid growth of music reality shows on Indian television; and (3) to debate whether reality shows are safer bets for launching talented singers and whether these singers can sustain their singing careers for long.

Baahubali: The Beginning – Digital Marketing Strategies [Case code: 516-0108-1]

Abstract:

This case study is meant to highlight how innovative marketing campaigns can enhance a product's (in this case Baahubali: The Beginning (Baahubali), the movie) market success. With carefully crafted and meticulously executed marketing strategies, with the same precision and finesse as that of the movie itself, Baahubali's market fortunes soared. With INR600 crore gross earnings worldwide, Baahubali not only became a benchmark for technical and aesthetic prowess, but also became a well-studied case for its marketing blitzkrieg. With 4 years of filming, thousands of artists, unprecedented sets and costumes, Baahubali's success opened new vistas in digital marketing for Indian movies. While the lead actors became national icons with big-brand endorsements, the film's crew including its director became sought after film technicians nationally and globally. An interesting feature of Baahubali's marketing campaign has been the value-chain approach in marketing the movie. As many industry veterans point out, nearly 40% of Baahubali's commercial success can be attributed to its aggressive and innovative marketing campaigns. What are the critical elements of Baahubali's marketing, especially WRT digital marketing campaign? What's the unique approach that Baahubali has adopted to sustain and accentuate its success? How could omni-channel marketing approach aid the movie's success? How could Baahubali's team orchestrate well-crafted brand-building strategies?

PVR Cinemas: Competitive Strategies of the Indian Cineplex Pioneer* [Case Code: COM0118]

Abstract:

Priya Village Roadshow (PVR) is the largest cinema exhibition player in India, which introduced the concept of multiplexes in the country in 1997 and redefined the movie viewing experience of the Indian audience. In 2004, the company also diversified into movie distribution. With many firsts to its credit, PVR opened multiplexes in the National Capital Region (NCR) of India and other metros like Mumbai, Bangalore and Hyderabad in 2006. However, since the turn of the 21st century, PVR has been facing stiff competition from other players, who have equal investment capabilities and similar expansion plans.

Pedagogical Objectives:

* To understand the movie exhibition business in India and the factors that led to the inception of the multiplex concept in India

* To discuss the growth strategies of PVR in the Indian multiplex business

* To analyse the competitive strategies of PVR's competitors and debate on strategies that might support PVR to sustain its leadership in the Indian multiplex industry.

*** available with ibscdc.org**

LOWE'S, AMD, TARGET ET AL: The Second-Mover Advantage? [Case Reference: 306-329-1]

Abstract:

In the world of business, the pioneer or the first-mover in an industry often fails to stand up to the competition from its follower or the second-mover due to its failure to constantly innovate, or to take timely and effective competitive decisions. The first-movers tend to cling on to their time-tested strategies, which yield positive results when they are the sole entity in a particular market - a phenomenon known as active inertia. This leads to a decline in their financial position and sometimes puts their existence in jeopardy. The second-movers, on the other hand, have been found to gain from the experiences of the pioneer and take full advantage of the pioneer's weaknesses and strategic mistakes. The teaching objectives are: (1) to understand the challenges that a pioneer faces in any industry and the factors that determine the sustainability of its leadership; (2) to analyse the various constraints of the first-movers, which are taken advantage of by the second-movers to strengthen their positions; and (3) to discuss how the first-movers can protect their lead in an industry, by keeping competition at bay.

The Namesake: The Success Recipe of an Indian Crossover Movie* **[Case Reference: RW-12]**

Abstract:

The case study speaks of the key factors that contributed to the success of the Mira Nair directed movie The Namesake both at the national as well as at the international box-office. Apart from having a globally thought provoking content, the movie was marketed with lots of innovation. The article also throws ample light on how movies mould the consumer behaviour of the cine audiences. The case can serve as a thought provoking discussion material in classes on consumer behaviour and business strategy.

*available at my blog mentioned

MojoPac: Redefining Mobile Computing? **[Case Reference: 307-085-1]**

Abstract:

In September 2006, California-based RingCube Technologies released its mobile computing software, MojoPac worldwide. The software could be installed on any device that had a universal serial bus (USB) port like iPod, USB key-chain drive, mobile phone or any gismo with digital storage space that was termed a Mojo device after the software installation. The technology behind the software enabled a user to work in a customised computing environment any place any time. It seemed that MojoPac, through its portability and enhanced security features, simplified the concept of mobile computing, a concept that the world was introduced to with the advent of laptops in the 1980s. The case is structured to: (1) analyse the evolution of mobile computing devices over the years; (2) understand and analyse the technology behind the MojoPac software; and (3) analyse the competitive scenario in the global mobile computing software industry.

Chak De! India: A Sustainable Trendsetter or an Ephemeral Euphoria? * **[Case Reference: RW-17]**

Abstract:

The case speaks of movies as not just a reflector of the society but also debates the impact of movies on the societal behaviour. In this context, the case has focused on Chak De! India, a movie starring Bollywood mega star Shah Rukh Khan, which was released in August 2007. It was found that the movie not only created awareness for hockey in India but also moulded the society's behaviour towards hockey as a sport. However, it was felt by many that the change was just a fad which was destined to die a natural death in due course of time. The case is appropriate for being discussed in classes on consumer behaviour and media studies.

*available at my blog mentioned

PepsiCo's `Youngistaan' Advertisement: Another Trendsetter in the Youth Marketing Arena* **[Case Code: MMAD10807]**

Abstract:

With the launch of the Youngistaan advertisement in early 2008, PepsiCo has proved once again its strong orientation towards the Indian youth. Since its first television commercial in 1989, PepsiCo has come up with innovative advertising campaigns that have gone on to become trendsetters. Its slogans have become much-sought-after catchphrases among the Indian youth. Over the years, PepsiCo has used in its advertisements, a galaxy of celebrities, having a huge fan following among the youth. Thus, we have had celebrities like Shah Rukh Khan, Juhi Chawla, Sachin Tendulkar and even Amitabh Bachchan endorsing the Cola brand. From `Yehi Hai Right Choice Baby' to `Yeh Hai Youngistaan Meri Jaan', PepsiCo has been spot on with its youth marketing endeavors.

*available with http://www.iupindia.in

power point presentation of case highlighting objectives and solutions

Winner of India Radio Forum Awards for the Best on-ground initiative

Entry Title: Ganesha Goes Green with "BIG Green Ganesha"

Background:

For the 4th year running, 92.7 BIG FM took up the initiative of Green celebrations on Ganesh Chaturthi. Various reports by government bodies and NGOs have revealed the adverse Ecological Impact that immersing non eco friendly Ganesha's statues in rivers causes. The POP and the harmful colors used in making of the idols not only make the water non potable but also badly affect the flora and fauna of the water body. Realizing this evil BIG FM constituted the property **'the BIG Green Ganesha'.** The promise of this property is to make encourage people to use Eco friendly ganesha and the ill effects of using a non 'green' idol

The genesis of the property lies in the company philosophy of "Suno Sunayoo Life Banayoo" i.e. positively affecting people through our station.

With each subsequent year the property has grown in scale covering 14 cities in 2011. With time this property has become synonymous with Ganpathi Pujan with listeners waiting for the subsequent leg of the campaign to kick start every year so that they can make their contribution to the environment

The Objective:

1) To spread the green message to the listeners and bring about a social consciousness
2) To build awareness and visibility for BIG FM's property "Green Ganesha" through On ground activation
3) Get the listeners involved with the property through the donation of paper and then crating the Ganesha out of it
4) To increase the listenership of BIG FM

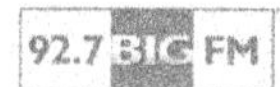

The Insight: **"Lord Ganpathi is sacred to all and contributing to making the Ganpathi brings about an instant connect"**

The Campaign:

Big Green Ganesha 2011 was the 4th year of the property and was executed across 14 stations namely Mumbai, Bangalore, Hyderabad, Chennai, Indore, Surat, Bhopal, Goa, Gwalior, Sholapur, Baroda, Vizag, Mysore, and Mangalore.

This was a Multiphase campaign involving

- On Air the RJs asking the listeners to take the pledge for using eco friendly ganesha's and also communicate the benefits of using eco friendly idols
- The listeners are then asked to donate waste paper. We sent out teams to collect the waste paper from households in each of the 14 cities.
- The waste paper is then converted into a Green Ganesha idol and installed in a pandal at a high footfall area.
- For the 9 days of ganpathi this idol is worshiped and the Listeners are encouraged to come to the blessings of the Lord.
- The pandals are visited by a host of celebrities and dignitaries across cities
- A Visarjan is done of the idol at the end of the 9 day festival

On Air Integrations:

- Listeners were asked to call in and pledge their support for the Campaign
- The route of the on ground team going for paper collection was announced on air and people were asked to donate paper
- The bytes collected from the people donating the newspaper on ground were played the next day on air
- The final kgs of paper collected was announced on air informing and thanking Listeners for their contribution
- The location of the final idol when installed was announced on air and listeners encouraged to seek the blessings of the Green Ganesha
- Every celebrity /dignitary visiting the pandal was announced on air and then their bytes supporting the campaign was played

Result of the campaign:

- The activity achieved immense response with more than 35000 people donating paper and covering 15000 households
- 8000 kgs of paper was collected
- Avg height of the paper ganesha in the 14 cities was 4 ft .
- The activity saw 14+ lakh people visiting the pandals across the cities
- PR worth crores was generated through the campaign increasing brand visibility

Supporting Photographs

Record paper collection

Multiple idols – One message

Celebs worship the Eco Friendly Ganpathi

Unprecedented Crowd Connect

Visarjan – the eco friendly way

*case study courtesy afaqs.com

About the author

Dr. Kisholoy Roy is a Ph.D. in Management from IIT (Indian School of Mines), Dhanbad, one of the premier education brands in India. He is an Accredited Management Teacher certified by All India Management Association (AIMA), New Delhi. Roy did his Masters in Business Administration (MBA) in Marketing from Visva-Bharati University, Santiniketan, one of the central universities in India.

Dr. Roy has authored several publications that include case studies, articles, research papers and books. He has been considered a subject matter expert in the domains of brand communication, retail marketing and sales.

Apart from this book Dr. Kisholoy Roy has authored titles themed on case studies like *How to Write and Teach Case Studies Effectively?* and also *Case Studies for Marketing Students*; both have been phenomenal sellers in the online marketplace like amazon, kobo, lulu, flipkart, kindle, createspace and pothi.

www.ingramcontent.com/pod-product-compliance
Lightning Source LLC
Chambersburg PA
CBHW061223180526
45170CB00003B/1127